For permission requests, please contact Olga Gerogianni at info@smallbusinessadvisor.uk

Disclaimer: The information provided in this ebook is for general informational purposes only. While every effort has been made to ensure the accuracy and completeness of the contents, the author assumes no responsibility for errors or omissions, or for any outcomes resulting from the use of the information provided. The author disclaims any liability for the actions or decisions made based on the information contained in this ebook. The reader is solely responsible for their own actions and should seek professional advice before starting or operating a micro business.

Acknowledgements: This ebook is a culmination of my 20 years of experience in entrepreneurship and my studies in Business Management at the Open University in Scotland. I am grateful to all the mentors, fellow entrepreneurs, and industry professionals who have shaped my journey and contributed to my knowledge and understanding of the business world. Their insights and support have been invaluable in the creation of this ebook.

Cover design: Olga Gerogianni Editor: Olga Gerogianni

Special thanks to my husband Spiros and my sons Achilleas and Aggelos for their unwavering support and encouragement throughout this writing process. Your belief in me and my passion for helping new entrepreneurs has been instrumental in bringing this ebook to life.

I dedicate this ebook to all aspiring and ambitious individuals who are ready to embark on their own entrepreneurial journey. May it provide you with the guidance, inspiration, and practical knowledge you need to navigate the challenges and achieve success in your micro business.

Contents

To my entrepreneurial family in Scotland, the passionate local traders at the markets, who brave all weather conditions to create, design, produce, sell, and provide unwavering customer support. Your hard work and resilience inspire us all.

Introduction

Welcome to "Start and Succeed," a comprehensive guide designed to help aspiring entrepreneurs navigate the journey of starting a small business. Whether you have a unique idea or want to create something innovative in a saturated market, this book will provide you with essential steps and valuable insights to turn your entrepreneurial dreams into a reality. Written by Olga Gerogianni, a seasoned business advisor with years of experience, this book combines practical advice, strategic thinking, and real-life examples to guide you through the process of building a successful small business.

"Hello there! I'm Olga, a 45-year-old mum, entrepreneur, and author of this ebook. I'm thrilled to have the opportunity to share my knowledge and experiences with you, and guide you on your journey to creating a successful brand.

Life has a way of throwing unexpected challenges our way, but I firmly believe that with determination, resilience, and the right mindset, we can overcome anything. As a mum, I've experienced the joys and responsibilities of raising a family, and I understand the unique dynamics that come with it. One of my boys has Down syndrome, which has taught me the importance of empathy, patience, and embracing diversity.

At the age of 40, I decided to embark on a new adventure by pursuing a degree in Business Management at Open University. This decision allowed me to deepen my knowledge in the field of entrepreneurship and further fuel my passion for building successful businesses. It was a transformative experience that showed me that age is just a number and it's never too late to pursue your dreams.

Additionally, I had the opportunity to change my life completely when I made the bold decision to move to a new country. Starting from scratch in a new environment was both challenging and exhilarating. It tested my resilience, adaptability, and determination. But through it all, I learned that with the right mindset and a clear vision, we can create new beginnings and achieve remarkable things.

Drawing from my personal journey, as well as my experiences as the founder of Estia Soaps, and the mistakes from the past with my two previous businesses, I wrote this ebook with the intention of inspiring and empowering fellow entrepreneurs like yourself. I want to show you that despite the challenges and obstacles that may come your way, you have the strength and ability to create a thriving business and a meaningful brand.

In this ebook, you'll find practical advice, actionable strategies, and real-life examples to help you navigate the exciting world of entrepreneurship. I share my insights on everything from identifying your passions and turning them into a successful business venture, to creating a memorable brand, harnessing the power of social media, and establishing a strong online presence.

I understand firsthand the juggling act of managing a business while being a dedicated parent. I know the importance of finding a balance and carving out time for both your family and your entrepreneurial pursuits. Throughout this ebook, I provide practical tips and guidance that can help you navigate these challenges and create a harmonious synergy between your personal and professional life.

So, whether you're a parent, a late bloomer, or someone who is seeking a fresh start, I want you to know that anything is possible. With determination, resilience, and the right knowledge, you can create a business that aligns with your passions, values, and goals.

Join me on this transformative journey as we explore the keys to building a successful brand, and let's prove that with the right mindset and a dose of courage, you can turn your dreams into reality.

Wishing you boundless inspiration and success on your entrepreneurial journey".

With love,

Olga

Common Mistakes in Micro Business: A Guide to Avoiding Pitfalls

Starting a micro business can be an exciting endeavour, but it's important to be aware of the common mistakes that new entrepreneurs often make. In this guide, we'll highlight the pitfalls that can hinder your success and growth. By understanding these challenges, you can take proactive steps to avoid them and increase your chances of building a thriving brand.

1. **Confusing Business with a Side Hustle or Hobby:**
   One of the most prevalent mistakes is treating a business like a side hustle or hobby. Unlike a hobby, a business requires serious investment and a focus on generating profits. Failure to recognize this difference can lead to financial losses and a lack of progress.
2. **Overlooking the Real Target Audience:**
   Relying solely on family and friends as customers is a common error. While their support is valuable, they may not represent your target audience. Neglecting to reach out to a broader customer base can hinder growth and limit long-term success.
3. **Unrealistic Expectations of Quick Wealth:**
   New entrepreneurs often believe that success will come quickly, but the reality is that building a profitable business takes time. Overestimating short-term gains can lead to disappointment and financial strain.
4. **Reliance on Inadequate Advice Sources:**
   Seeking advice from friends, family, and random entrepreneurial groups without professional guidance can lead to poor decision-making. Without the

expertise of a dedicated business advisor, you risk making choices that may not align with the realities of the business world.

5. **Lack of Planning and Spontaneous Decision-making**:
   Starting a business without proper planning and strategic decision-making can result in a weak brand identity, a lack of customer trust, and an ineffective market presence. Avoiding careful consideration can hinder growth and jeopardize long-term success.

6. **Failure to Differentiate Personal and Business on Social Media:**
   Blurring the lines between personal and business social media accounts is a common misstep. Failing to create separate profiles can dilute your brand image and confuse potential customers, hindering your professional reputation.

7. **Insufficient Budget Allocation:**
   Starting with limited resources is typical for micro businesses, but making poor financial choices can have lasting consequences. Neglecting to invest in professional branding and opting for cheap alternatives can undermine your brand's credibility and hinder customer engagement.

8. **Inaccurate Product Cost Calculation:**
   Ignoring the importance of accurately calculating product costs can result in misleading profit margins and financial setbacks. Failing to factor in all expenses, including materials, packaging, and labelling, can lead to pricing errors and ultimately, loss-making sales.

9. **Failure to Utilize Wholesale Channels:**
   Neglecting to explore partnerships with wholesalers for sourcing supplies can limit profitability. By not taking advantage of bulk order discounts, you miss out on potential cost savings that could enhance your profit margins.

10. **Neglecting Quality Customer Service:**
    Failing to prioritize exceptional customer service can negatively impact customer satisfaction and retention. Treating customers casually, without the necessary respect and professionalism, can damage your reputation and hinder long-term growth.

By being aware of these common mistakes, you can take proactive measures to avoid them and set your micro business on a path to success.

Welcome to "Start and Succeed," a comprehensive guide designed to help aspiring entrepreneurs navigate the journey of starting a small business. Whether you have a unique idea or want to create something innovative in a saturated market, this book will provide you with essential steps and valuable insights to turn your entrepreneurial dreams into a reality. Written by Olga Gerogianni, a seasoned business advisor with years of experience, this book combines practical advice, strategic thinking, and real-life examples to guide you through the process of building a successful small business.

✓ **Chapter 1**: **To Be an Entrepreneur - Think Like an Entrepreneur**

Being an entrepreneur requires a different perspective and mindset. As a first-time business owner, it's important to change your mindset and embrace the entrepreneurial perspective. This includes:

1. **Seeing opportunities everywhere:**
   Entrepreneurs possess the ability to spot potential business opportunities in various situations. They train themselves to identify untapped markets, unmet needs, and innovative solutions that others may overlook. It's about thinking creatively and uncovering hidden possibilities.
2. **Engaging in brainstorming and generating new ideas:**
   Entrepreneurs actively foster their creativity and constantly seek new ideas. They understand that innovation is the lifeblood of a successful business. By encouraging brainstorming sessions and embracing fresh concepts, entrepreneurs keep their ventures dynamic and stay ahead of the competition.
3. **Taking calculated risks and planning ahead:**
   Entrepreneurs are not afraid to take risks, but they do so with careful consideration. They understand the importance of planning ahead, conducting thorough research, and making informed decisions. By weighing the potential rewards against the risks involved, entrepreneurs increase their chances of success.
4. **Embracing market research:**
   Market research becomes an inherent part of an entrepreneur's journey. It's not just a task to be done but a constant habit. Successful entrepreneurs stay attuned to changing customer demands, evolving trends, and their competitors' offerings. This knowledge empowers them to adapt their strategies and stay relevant in a dynamic marketplace.
5. **Embracing the entrepreneurial lifestyle:**
   Entrepreneurship is more than just a pursuit of financial gains. It's about embracing a lifestyle that offers flexibility, endless opportunities for growth, and the freedom to manifest one's creative vision. However, entrepreneurs are also aware of the downsides. They understand that failures, financial setbacks, and the need to work longer hours than employees are part of the journey. Entrepreneurs often prioritize paying their employees and suppliers before themselves, demonstrating their commitment and responsibility.

By incorporating these perspectives into their mindset, aspiring entrepreneurs can navigate the entrepreneurial landscape more effectively. They understand that entrepreneurship is a multifaceted journey that combines financial aspirations with the pursuit of creativity, flexibility, and the realization of untapped opportunities. They are prepared to face the challenges that come with it, such as failures and financial risks, while embracing the rewards that make the journey worthwhile.

Case study Estia soaps

As you already know, I am the founder of Estia Soaps Ltd. I have always been passionate about natural skincare products and wanted to share my love for handmade soaps with others. With a strong entrepreneurial mindset, I identified a gap in the market for high-quality, organic soaps that align with eco-conscious values. I later expanded the range of products to aromatherapy, bath and skincare.

Key Selling Points:

1. 100% Natural: Estia Soaps prides itself on using only natural ingredients in its soap formulations. Customers can trust that the products are free from harsh chemicals and synthetic additives.
2. Vegan-Friendly and Cruelty-Free: The soaps are vegan-friendly, meaning they contain no animal-derived ingredients and are not tested on animals. This appeals to individuals who follow a vegan lifestyle and value cruelty-free products.
3. Plastic-Free Packaging: Estia Soaps is committed to reducing plastic waste. The packaging is environmentally friendly, using materials like biodegradable paper or recyclable containers, minimizing the impact on the environment.
4. Handmade with Care: Each soap bar is meticulously handcrafted, ensuring attention to detail and quality. This handmade process adds a personal touch and showcases the dedication of the brand to deliver exceptional products.
5. Multifunctional and Minimalist Approach: Estia Soaps products, are designed to work in a multifunctional way, offering benefits beyond basic cleansing. For example, some soaps can be used for body, face, and hair, reducing the need for multiple products and minimizing the carbon footprint.

By emphasizing these key selling points, Estia Soaps positions itself as a brand that not only offers high-quality natural skincare products but also aligns with the values and preferences of eco-conscious consumers. This differentiation sets Estia Soaps apart from competitors and resonates with customers who prioritize sustainability and ethical choices in their skincare routine.

Here's a small exercise for you.

Visit a local market with handmade products and this time focus on the products from an entrepreneur's perspective. Choose three products that are appealing to you, and mark down for each one:

➢ *Why it dragged your attention? (Packaging? Price? Branding? Uniqueness?)*

➢ *Is the retail price reasonable? (Consider the costs of the product till the packaging)*

➢ *Would you buy it? (The price fulfils a need. And if yes, would you buy it regularly? Or if no, why?)*

What do you see?

Notes

product 1

product 2

product 3

Now take time to identify similar products online and compare them. Once you find the same but at a better price, what is the main difference? Is it on the packaging, or the ingredients or something else? What would you make different?

✓ **Chapter 2: Your business idea**

Identifying your interests and skills is a crucial step in creating a business that aligns with your passions and strengths. Here's a step-by-step guide on how to identify your interests and skills and turn them into a successful business venture:

1. **Self-Reflection:**
   Take time to reflect on your personal interests and hobbies. What activities do you enjoy doing in your free time? What subjects or industries fascinate you? Consider the things that bring you joy and fulfilment.

2. **Skills Assessment:**
   Evaluate your skills and strengths. What are you naturally good at? What knowledge or expertise have you acquired through education, training, or work experience? Identify both technical skills (e.g., graphic design, programming) and soft skills (e.g., communication, leadership) that you possess.

3. **Market Research:**
   Explore the market to identify opportunities where your interests and skills can be applied. Look for gaps or underserved areas in the market that align with your passions and expertise. Research potential target customers, competitors, and trends in your chosen industry.

4. **Idea Generation:**
   Brainstorm business ideas that leverage your interests and skills. Consider how you can solve a problem or meet a need in the market using your unique strengths. Explore different business models and identify potential products or services that align with your passion and expertise.

5. **Validation:**
   Once you have a list of business ideas, validate them by gathering feedback from potential customers, mentors, or industry experts. Seek their opinions and insights to determine the viability and market demand for your ideas.

6. **Refinement:**
   Based on the feedback received, refine your business ideas and narrow down your options. Focus on the ideas that have the most potential for success and align closely with your interests and skills.

7. **Business Plan:**
   Develop a comprehensive business plan that outlines your business concept, target market, marketing strategies, financial projections, and operational details. This plan will serve as a roadmap for your business and help you stay organized and focused.

8. **Skill Enhancement:**
   If you identify any gaps in your skills or knowledge required for your chosen business, consider acquiring additional training or education. Attend workshops, take online courses, or seek mentorship to enhance your capabilities.

9. **Implementation:**
   Take action and start building your business. Set up the necessary infrastructure, such as creating a website, establishing a brand identity, and securing any required licenses or permits. Begin marketing your products or services and start engaging with potential customers.

10. **Continuous Learning and Adaptation:**
    As you launch your business, be open to learning from your experiences and adapting your strategies. Stay informed about industry trends, seek customer feedback, and continuously refine your offerings to meet the evolving needs of your target market.

Remember, creating a business based on your interests and skills increases your chances of success and brings a sense of fulfilment and passion to your entrepreneurial journey. Embrace your unique talents and pursue your entrepreneurial dreams with confidence.

Case study: Estia soaps Ltd

Identifying my interests and skills was a crucial step in creating a business that aligns with my passions and strengths. Let me share with you my journey of turning my interests and skills into a successful business venture.

1. **Self-Reflection:**
   I took the time to reflect on my personal interests and hobbies. I've always had a deep love for skincare and a passion for natural and sustainable living. These activities brought me joy and a sense of fulfilment. It took me 13 years of experiments for the final soap recipes, and I was working on the branding for up to a year.
2. **Skills Assessment:**
   I evaluated my skills and strengths. With a background in Spa industry and a knack for creating homemade skincare products, I knew I had the technical skills to develop high-quality, natural skincare solutions. Additionally, my strong communication and customer service skills were an asset for building relationships with customers.
3. **Market Research:**
   I delved into market research to identify opportunities where my interests and skills could be applied. After all I was in a new country with different habits and shopping choices. I discovered a growing demand for eco-friendly skincare products that were both effective and sustainable. I also identified a gap for olive oil-based products in the UK. Through research, I gained insights into potential target customers, competitors, and emerging trends in the natural skincare industry.
4. **Idea Generation:**
   I brainstormed business ideas that leveraged my interests and skills. I envisioned creating a line of handmade, all-natural soaps that were not only gentle on the skin but also eco-friendly and multifunctional. These soaps would be crafted using organic ingredients and packaged sustainably, aligning with my commitment to the environment.
5. **Validation:**
   I sought feedback from potential customers, mentors, and industry experts to validate my business ideas. Their positive responses and enthusiasm

confirmed the market demand for eco-conscious skincare products and provided valuable insights for further refinement.

6. **Refinement:**
Based on the feedback received, I refined my business ideas and narrowed down my options. I focused on developing a range of all-natural soaps with unique scents and skin-nourishing properties. This refinement process helped me align my offerings more closely with customer preferences.

7. **Business Plan:**
I developed a comprehensive business plan that outlined my business concept, target market, marketing strategies, financial projections, and operational details. This plan served as a roadmap, guiding me through the various aspects of my business and ensuring I stayed organized and focused.

8. **Skill Enhancement:**
Recognizing the need to enhance my skills further, I attended workshops and online courses on soap-making techniques, product formulation, and sustainable packaging. This additional training allowed me to elevate the quality of my products and develop a strong brand identity.

9. **Implementation:**
I took action and started building my business. I created a website that showcased my handmade soaps, established a brand identity that reflected my values, and obtained the necessary licenses and permits. Through targeted marketing efforts, I began engaging with potential customers and building a loyal customer base.

10. **Continuous Learning and Adaptation:**
As I launched my business, I remained open to learning from my experiences and adapting my strategies. I kept myself informed about industry trends, actively sought customer feedback, and continuously refined my product offerings to meet the evolving needs of my target market. During the pandemic I identified the need of people to spend more time at home, and created a new collection based on the power of aromatherapy, creating a spa-at-home experience.

*What no one will tell you about finding a business idea: Look for problems to solve rather than focusing solely on your passions. A business that solves a problem has a higher chance of success.

✓ **Chapter 3: Is Your Idea Already in the Market?**

The Importance of Continuous Market Research
Conducting an online search: Start by searching online as if you were a potential customer. Use relevant keywords and phrases to find products or services similar to what you plan to offer. This will help you understand the existing market landscape and identify your potential competitors.

Competitor Analysis
Examining competitors: Visit the websites, physical stores, or online marketplaces where your competitors sell their products or services. Take note of their offerings, pricing, product features, and any unique selling points they highlight. Pay attention

to how they present their products, the quality of their packaging, and their overall branding.

Assessing Packaging, Pricing, and Unique Selling Points

Analyzing products and services: Purchase items from your competitors to gain firsthand experience with their products or services. Evaluate the quality, functionality, and customer experience they provide. Consider what you like about their offerings and what you believe could be improved or differentiated in your own business.

Customer Experience Evaluation

Assessing customer service: Interact with your competitors' customer service representatives, either in-person, via phone, or through online channels. Take note of their responsiveness, knowledge, and overall customer experience. This will help you understand the level of service customers expect and identify ways to provide even better customer support in your own business.

Utilizing Google and Online Tools

Reviewing website presentation: Explore your competitors' websites and analyze their design, layout, and user experience. Consider how easy it is to navigate, find information, and make purchases. Pay attention to the visuals, product descriptions, and any customer reviews or testimonials they feature. This will provide insights into effective website strategies and help you create a user-friendly and visually appealing website for your own business.

Identifying unique selling points: Look for the unique features, benefits, or values that set your competitors apart. These could be eco-friendly practices, 24/7 customer support, customization options, or any other aspects that make them stand out. Understanding their unique selling points will help you determine how you can differentiate your own business and provide added value to customers.

By conducting thorough market research, you'll gain valuable insights into the competitive landscape, understand customer expectations, and identify opportunities to position your business uniquely. This information will guide your business decisions, product development, marketing strategies, and overall business growth.

*What no one will tell you about market research:
Don't just rely on online research. Get out there and talk to potential customers,
attend industry events, and gather real-world insights.

✓ **Chapter 4: Decide What YOU Will Do -Why customers should buy from you?**

Differentiating Your Product or Service

Consider the benefits: Identify the unique advantages and value your product or service offers compared to competitors. Highlight how it solves a problem or meets a specific need of your target audience. Focus on the customer: Understand that your customer should be the central focus of your product or service. Consider their needs, desires, and pain points when developing your offering. By putting yourself in their shoes, you can create a solution that truly resonates with them.

1. **Ethical values:** If your target audience values sustainability, fair trade, or other ethical considerations, emphasize how your product/service aligns with these values.
2. **Pricing:** Determine your pricing strategy, considering factors such as production costs, competitor pricing, and the perceived value of your offering. Aim to strike a balance between affordability and profitability. Pricing plays a crucial role in differentiating your product or service. Calculate your costs accurately, including materials, production, overhead, and any additional expenses. Determine a fair and competitive price that not only covers your costs but also allows for a reasonable profit margin. Consider the perceived value of your offering and how it compares to similar products or services in the market.

Unique selling points: Identify aspects of your product/service that set it apart from the competition. This could include innovative features, superior quality, exceptional customer service, or any other attributes that make your offering stand out.

3. **Determining sales channels:**
- Website: Consider establishing an online presence through a dedicated e-commerce website. This allows your target audience to purchase directly from you and provides a platform for showcasing your products/services.
- Local markets: Explore opportunities to participate in local markets or fairs relevant to your target audience. This can help you reach potential customers in person and build brand awareness.
- Social media platforms: Leverage popular social media platforms that align with your target audience's preferences. Create engaging content, share updates, and interact with your audience to generate interest and drive sales.
- Physical shops: If suitable for your target audience, consider setting up a brick-and-mortar store in a location frequented by your potential customers.
- Wholesale channels: Explore partnerships with retailers or distributors who can sell your products/services on your behalf. This can help you reach a wider customer base and increase sales volume.

4. **Considering space requirements:**
- If your business involves physical products, assess the storage and operational space needed. Ensure you have enough room to store inventory, assemble products, and fulfill orders efficiently. This may require renting or purchasing a suitable workspace.

5. **Identifying suppliers:**
- Research and identify reliable suppliers who can provide the necessary materials or services for your business. Consider factors such as quality, pricing, delivery times, and their ability to meet your business's specific needs.

6. **Defining your ideal customers:**

- Determine the characteristics of your target audience, including age group, interests, and localization. Conduct market research or create customer personas to gain a deeper understanding of their needs, preferences, and buying behavior.
- Tailor your marketing efforts accordingly to effectively reach and engage your target audience. This includes crafting relevant messaging, selecting appropriate marketing channels, and creating compelling content that resonates with your ideal customers.

Remember, differentiation is not just about standing out from competitors but also about providing value to your customers. By understanding their needs, addressing their pain points, and offering something unique and compelling, you can create a strong differentiation strategy that sets your business apart in the marketplace.

By following these instructions, you can effectively differentiate your product or service, determine the appropriate sales channels, meet space requirements, identify reliable suppliers, and tailor your marketing efforts to your target audience's characteristics. This will help position your business for success and attract the right customers for your offering.

Case study Estia soaps:

Let me share my own experience with Estia Soaps and how I differentiated my product to attract customers. At Estia Soaps, we are passionate about creating natural, vegan-friendly, and eco-conscious skincare products that leave a positive impact on both our customers and the environment.

One of the key factors that set us apart from competitors is our commitment to ethical values. We believe in sustainability and reducing our carbon footprint, which is why all our products are plastic-free and handmade using only 100% natural ingredients. This resonates with our target audience who value eco-friendly and cruelty-free options.

Another important aspect we focused on was pricing. We wanted to offer products that were not only high-quality but also affordable. By carefully calculating our costs, including materials, production, and overhead expenses, we were able to determine a fair and competitive price that covered our costs and allowed for a reasonable profit margin. This helped us attract price-conscious customers who appreciated the value we provided.

To reach our customers effectively, we utilized various sales channels. Our e-commerce website served as a central hub where customers could easily browse and purchase our products. We also actively engaged with our audience through social media platforms like Instagram and Facebook, sharing engaging content, running giveaways, and responding to customer inquiries. Additionally, we participated in local markets and fairs to connect with customers in person and build brand awareness.

By identifying our unique selling points, considering customer needs, and utilizing various sales channels, we were able to create a strong position in the market. Customers choose Estia Soaps not only for our high-quality, eco-friendly products but also because they resonate with our values and appreciate the personalized customer experience we provide.

> *What no one will tell you about creating a unique value proposition: Focus on the specific benefits your product or service offers, rather than just listing features. Clearly communicate how your offering solves a problem or fulfills a need better than competitors.*

Notes

My business idea

**Why my idea is
different?**

✓ **Chapter 5: Identifying Your Target Audience - Connecting with the Right Customers**

One of the common pitfalls for new micro business owners is the misconception that their customer base solely consists of friends and family. While their support is valuable, it's essential to recognize that your target audience extends beyond this close circle. To effectively reach and engage customers, it's crucial to identify your true target audience – those who align with the benefits and values your product or service provides.

1. **Benefits and Value Proposition:**
   Start by understanding the unique advantages and value your offering brings to customers. Consider the problem it solves or the need it fulfils. Is it a luxury product that offers exclusivity and premium quality? Does it focus on sustainability and appeal to eco-conscious individuals? Is it affordable and caters to a cost-conscious demographic? By identifying the benefits and value proposition, you can pinpoint the audience segment that would find your product/service most appealing.
2. **Branding and Positioning:**
   Your brand identity plays a vital role in attracting the right customers. Evaluate your branding elements, such as visual aesthetics, messaging, and brand voice. Does it resonate with a specific demographic or lifestyle? For example, minimalist and modern branding may attract younger, urban consumers, while a vintage-inspired aesthetic might appeal to a nostalgic audience. Define your brand personality and ensure it aligns with the preferences and aspirations of your target audience.
3. **Demographic and Psychographic Characteristics**:
4. Conduct market research to understand the demographics and psychographics of your potential customers. Demographics include factors such as age, gender, location, income level, and occupation, while psychographics delve into interests, values, attitudes, and lifestyle choices. Analyze these aspects to create a comprehensive profile of your target audience. This will help you tailor your marketing efforts and communicate your brand's unique proposition effectively.
5. **Customer Surveys and Feedback:**
   Engage with your existing customers through surveys and feedback to gain insights into their preferences, motivations, and buying behaviors. Use this information to refine your target audience profile and understand what resonates with them. Additionally, leverage social media platforms and online communities to interact with potential customers and gather valuable feedback.
6. Competitor Analysis: Study your competitors who offer similar products or services. Analyze their target audience and identify any gaps or underserved segments in the market. This analysis can provide valuable insights into customer preferences and help you differentiate your business from the competition.

By taking the time to identify your target audience based on the benefits and value of your product or service, your branding, and various demographic and psychographic characteristics, you can refine your marketing efforts and connect with the right customers. Remember, understanding your audience is a continuous process, so always be open to feedback, adapt your strategies, and refine your approach to effectively reach and engage your target customers.

*What no one will tell you about building customer relationships: Focus on building genuine connections and providing exceptional customer service. Loyal customers can become your brand ambassadors. Maintain respect for your business and never present it as a side hustle. Build Trust and Consistency.

Notes

My ideal customer:

age range / gender:

Interests:

Location (where they live):

✓ **Chapter 6: Sales channels**

1. Selling physical in markets/local events:

Local markets offer an incredible opportunity for crafters and artisans to showcase their unique creations, connect with customers, and generate sales in a vibrant community setting. These markets serve as bustling hubs where individuals can discover one-of-a-kind handmade products, support local businesses, and engage in a personalized shopping experience. If you're a crafter looking to sell your products at these markets, here's what you need to know.

Finding Local Markets: Start by researching your local area for markets that align with your craft and target audience. Look for farmers' markets, artisan markets, craft fairs, or community events that welcome handmade products. Local newspapers, online directories, social media groups, and word-of-mouth recommendations can be excellent resources to identify potential markets in your vicinity.

Understanding Local Markets: Local markets are dynamic and diverse platforms that bring together a wide range of vendors offering various products and services. They often showcase handmade crafts, artisanal goods, farm-fresh produce, gourmet food items, and much more. These markets foster a sense of community, celebrate local talent, and provide an interactive space where customers can engage directly with sellers.

Minimizing Competition: When considering a local market, it's crucial to evaluate the presence of other crafters selling similar products. While a little competition can be healthy, it's generally advisable to avoid overcrowded markets where numerous vendors offer identical or closely resembling items. By ensuring there are no more than a couple of sellers offering the same products, you increase your chances of standing out and capturing the attention of potential customers.

By participating in local markets that align with your craft, you gain the opportunity to showcase your handmade creations, engage directly with customers, and build a loyal following within your community. Remember to embrace the uniqueness of your products, create an appealing display, and provide exceptional customer service to make a lasting impression. Let your creativity shine and enjoy the rewarding experience of connecting with customers who appreciate and support your craft.

To start selling at a market, it's important to have the following items and considerations:

1. **Public Liability Insurance**:

Ensure you have the appropriate insurance coverage, such as public liability insurance, to protect yourself and your business. Make sure to research and find the equivalent insurance requirements for your country.

2. **Display Setup:**
 Create an attractive and functional display for your products. Consider using portable shelves, crates, or any unique display ideas that showcase your items effectively.

3. **Price Tags and Product Information:**
Clearly label each product with price tags and provide informative boards that explain the product details. Take the opportunity to share your story behind the products and highlight key selling points, such as being handmade or vegan.

4. **Branded Tablecloth:**
Use a tablecloth that matches your branding to create a cohesive and professional look for your stall.

5. **Flyers and Business Cards:**
Have printed materials such as flyers and business cards available. Including a QR code leading to your website can be helpful since people may not always take physical flyers.

6. **Banners:**
 Use banners at the front and back of your stall to attract attention and showcase your brand. Consider hooks or other hanging solutions to secure the banners.

7. Decorations: Add decorative elements to your stall to create an inviting and visually appealing atmosphere that reflects your brand.

8. Card Machine: Invest in a portable card machine, such as Square, Zettle, or SumUp, for convenient and secure payment processing. These devices are easy to handle and carry.

9. Water: Bring water with you to stay hydrated, especially if there aren't any nearby coffee shops or drinking water sources available.

10. Table: Ensure that the market organizer provides a table for your stall. If not, bring a foldable table that suits your needs.

11. Avoiding Samples: Instead of offering small samples that customers can take with them, consider having testers available. This allows customers to instantly try or taste your products and can lead to higher conversion rates.

12. Carrier Trolley: Use a carrier trolley to help you transport your products and display materials to and from the market. It will make your setup and pack-up process much easier.

13. Rubber Mat: If you are in a cold country, consider bringing a rubber mat to place under your feet. It provides insulation and helps keep your feet warm in chilly weather.

Remember to adapt this list to your specific business needs and the regulations of the market you will be attending. Being well-prepared with these essentials will help you create an inviting and professional stall that attracts customers and enhances your selling experience.

2. **Establishing a Physical Store for Micro Businesses**

For micro businesses and new entrepreneurs, setting up a physical store can be an exciting step towards expanding their customer reach and creating a tangible presence in the market. However, it's important to recognize that operating a physical store demands a significant level of commitment. In this guide, we'll explore the essentials to consider when opening a physical store and emphasize the commitment required for its success.

Rent and Taxes: The first consideration is the cost of rent for the store space, along with any associated taxes or fees. Unlike other sales channels, a physical store requires a fixed location that requires regular payment. This financial commitment should align with your business's revenue and growth projections.

Utilities: Alongside rent, utilities such as electricity, water, and heating are ongoing expenses that require attention and consistent payment. Being accountable for utility bills adds to the commitment of running a physical store and must be factored into your financial planning.

Employee Costs: Hiring and managing employees further underscores the commitment involved in operating a physical store. Beyond the financial aspects, you'll need to dedicate time and effort to training, supervising, and creating a positive work environment. This commitment to your staff can significantly impact the success of your store.

Suppliers and Inventory: Maintaining inventory levels and nurturing relationships with suppliers are ongoing responsibilities for physical store owners. Regularly restocking shelves, managing stock levels, and ensuring timely deliveries demand consistent attention and commitment. Reliable suppliers are crucial for the smooth operation of your store.

Store Setup and Maintenance: Establishing a physical store requires an upfront commitment of time, effort, and financial resources. From designing the store layout to setting up fixtures and implementing an effective point-of-sale system, the initial setup process demands careful planning and execution. Additionally, ongoing store maintenance and occasional renovations will require your attention and dedication.

Operational Hours: Unlike online businesses or side hustles, physical stores typically have fixed operating hours. Commitment to being present and available during these hours is vital for providing customer service, building relationships, and generating sales. Being consistently available to customers establishes trust and loyalty, furthering the success of your store.

3. SELLING ONLINE

When deciding to start selling online, there are several options available to new entrepreneurs. Let's explore these options and discuss the pros and cons of each:

1. E-commerce Platforms:

Pros: User-friendly interface, pre-built website templates, integrated payment processing, customer support. Amazon, Etsy, Shopify are a good option to consider.

Cons: Monthly fees or transaction fees, limited customization options, competition within the platform.

2. Social Media Platforms:

Pros: Large user base, easy to set up and manage, potential for viral reach and engagement. Cons: Limited e-commerce features, may require additional tools for payment processing, less control over branding and customer experience.

3. Online Marketplaces:

Pros: Established customer base, built-in trust and credibility, marketing and exposure. Cons: Transaction fees and commission charges, limited customization options, increased competition.

4. Self-Hosted Websites:

Pros: Complete control over branding and customization, flexibility to scale and add features, and no transaction fees. Cons: Requires technical knowledge or hiring a web developer, additional costs for domain, hosting, and security, marketing and attracting traffic is the entrepreneur's responsibility.

5. Dropshipping:

Pros: No inventory management or upfront costs, wide product selection, flexibility to operate from anywhere. Cons: Lower profit margins, reliance on third-party suppliers and shipping, limited control over product quality and delivery times.

6. Print-on-Demand:

Pros: No inventory required, wide range of customizable products, low upfront costs. Cons: Limited profit margins, reliance on printing and fulfilment partners, longer delivery times.

7. Subscription Boxes:

Pros: Recurring revenue model, customer loyalty and engagement, potential for higher profit margins. Cons: Requires continuous product sourcing and curation, logistics and fulfilment challenges, and customer churn.

8. Mobile Apps:

Pros: Direct access to customers' mobile devices, enhanced user experience and personalization. Cons: Higher development and maintenance costs, platform-specific limitations, and lower discoverability compared to websites.

9. Online Services Platforms:

Pros: Access to a large customer base, streamlined service delivery and payment processing, customer reviews and ratings. Cons: Platform fees or commissions, competition from other service providers, limited control over pricing and customer relationships.

It's important to carefully evaluate each option based on your business model, target audience, and budget. Consider factors such as ease of use, customization options, scalability, costs, and the level of control and ownership you desire. Additionally, conduct market research to understand where your target audience prefers to shop online and which platforms align with your product or service.

23

Remember, it's often beneficial to diversify your online presence by leveraging multiple channels to reach a wider audience and mitigate risks associated with relying on a single platform.

*What no one will tell you about setting up operations: Streamline your processes and consider outsourcing certain tasks to free up time for strategic planning and business growth.

✓ **Chapter 7: SEO**

SEO, or Search Engine Optimization, is the practice of optimizing your online content to improve its visibility and ranking in search engine results pages (SERPs). It involves various strategies and techniques to increase organic (non-paid) traffic to your website or online platforms. SEO is crucial for businesses as it helps drive targeted traffic, increases brand visibility, and boosts online credibility. It connects different aspects of your online presence, including social media, website content, and image optimization, to improve your overall digital marketing efforts.

Importance of SEO:

1. Increased Visibility: Effective SEO ensures your website and content are visible to your target audience when they search for relevant keywords or phrases.
2. **Organic Traffic:** By optimizing your website for search engines, you can attract more organic traffic, resulting in higher chances of conversions and customer engagement.
3. **Brand Credibility:** Ranking higher in search results builds trust and credibility among users, as they perceive top-ranking websites as more authoritative and trustworthy.
4. **User Experience:** SEO techniques focus on enhancing the user experience, including fast page loading speeds, mobile optimization, and easy navigation, which leads to improved customer satisfaction and lower bounce rates.
5. **Cost-Effectiveness:** Compared to paid advertising, SEO provides a long-term and cost-effective solution for driving targeted traffic to your website.
6. **Competitive Advantage:** Implementing SEO strategies can help you outrank competitors and gain a competitive edge in your industry.

How to Apply SEO on Your Own:

1. **Keyword Research:** Identify relevant keywords and phrases that your target audience uses to search for products or services similar to yours. Use keyword research tools to discover popular and low-competition keywords.
2. **On-Page Optimization:** Optimize your website's meta tags, headings, and content with the identified keywords. Ensure the content is relevant, informative, and well-structured.

3. **Technical SEO:** Improve your website's technical aspects, such as page loading speed, mobile-friendliness, URL structure, and XML sitemap, to enhance search engine crawling and indexing.
4. **Link Building:** Earn high-quality backlinks from reputable websites to increase your website's authority and visibility. Focus on building natural and relevant links.
5. **Social Media Integration:** Share your website content on social media platforms to drive traffic, engagement, and social signals that can positively impact your SEO.
6. **Image Optimization:** Optimize image filenames, alt tags, and descriptions with relevant keywords to improve their visibility in image search results.
7. **Content Marketing:** Create valuable, shareable, and keyword-rich content that aligns with your target audience's interests and needs. Regularly update and optimize your content to keep it fresh and relevant.
8. **Analytics and Monitoring:** Use tools like Google Analytics to track your website's performance, keyword rankings, and user behavior. Monitor the results and make data-driven adjustments to your SEO strategies.

Pros of DIY SEO:

1. Cost-Effective: Implementing SEO strategies on your own can save money compared to hiring an SEO expert or agency.
2. Control and Flexibility: You have full control over the SEO tactics, implementation, and timeline.
3. Learning Opportunity: By delving into SEO practices, you gain valuable knowledge about digital marketing and can apply it to future projects.

Cons of DIY SEO:

1. Steep Learning Curve: SEO requires continuous learning and keeping up with industry updates, which can be time-consuming and challenging for beginners.
2. Time-Intensive: Implementing SEO strategies and monitoring results can take a significant amount of time, especially when managing other aspects of your business.
3. Limited Expertise: SEO is a complex field, and without professional guidance, you may miss out on advanced strategies or overlook important optimization opportunities.

Remember, while DIY SEO can be effective for small businesses, it's important to assess your expertise, available time, and the complexity of your SEO needs. Consider consulting with an SEO professional if you require specialized knowledge or if you have a larger budget to invest in comprehensive SEO services.

*What no one will tell you about keywords:

Keywords connect everything. They are the unsung heroes that fuel your online success. From product descriptions and image alt text to captivating social media posts, incorporating keywords strategically across all platforms is crucial. Unlock their power to boost visibility, attract your target audience, and establish a strong digital presence.

Here's an exercise to help you identify the keywords for your business. Write down up to 20 words that describe your product/service. Do the same for phrases. Think how your customer would search for what you are offering.

Notes

Main keywords (single words)

Secondary keywords (phrases)

Retail and wholesale are two distinct selling channels that businesses can utilize to reach their customers and distribute their products. Understanding the differences between these two channels, as well as their pros and cons, can help entrepreneurs make informed decisions about which approach best suits their business model. Let's delve into the details of each:

1. **Retail:** Retail involves selling products directly to the end consumer. This can take place through various avenues, such as brick-and-mortar stores, e-commerce platforms, or even pop-up shops. Here are some key characteristics and pros and cons of the retail channel:

Definition: Retail focuses on selling products in smaller quantities directly to individual consumers.

Pros of Retail:
- Direct customer interaction: Retail allows for direct engagement with customers, building relationships and providing personalized assistance.
- Higher profit margins: By selling directly to consumers, businesses can often charge higher prices, leading to increased profit margins.
- Flexibility in pricing and promotions: Retailers have the freedom to set their own prices and run promotional campaigns to attract customers.
- Brand exposure and customer loyalty: Retail stores provide an opportunity for customers to experience the brand firsthand, fostering brand loyalty and repeat business.

Cons of Retail:
- Higher operational costs: Operating retail stores involves expenses such as rent, utilities, and staffing, which can impact profitability.
- Inventory management challenges: Retailers need to manage inventory levels to meet customer demand while avoiding overstocking or stockouts.
- Intense competition: Retail is a highly competitive market, with numerous businesses vying for customers' attention and loyalty.

2. **Wholesale**:
Wholesale involves selling products in larger quantities to businesses or retailers, who then sell the products to end consumers. Here are the key characteristics and pros and cons of the wholesale channel:

Definition: Wholesale focuses on selling products in bulk to other businesses or retailers, rather than directly to consumers.

Pros of Wholesale:
- Larger sales volumes: Selling in bulk allows for larger order quantities, leading to higher sales volumes and potential revenue.
- Streamlined distribution: Working with wholesalers can simplify the distribution process for manufacturers, as they can reach a broader network of retailers.

- Cost savings: Wholesalers often offer discounted prices for bulk purchases, allowing businesses to save on per-unit costs.

Cons of Wholesale:

- Lower profit margins: Wholesale prices are typically lower than retail prices, which can result in lower profit margins for the manufacturer.
- Limited control over branding and customer experience: As products are sold to other businesses, manufacturers have less control over how their brand is represented or the customer experience provided.
- Dependence on wholesale partners: Success in the wholesale channel relies on building and maintaining strong relationships with wholesalers, which can be challenging.

Ultimately, the choice between retail and wholesale depends on the nature of the business, target market, and overall strategy. Some businesses may opt for a combination of both channels, leveraging the advantages of each to maximize sales and reach a wider customer base.

As a new entrepreneur, deciding between retail and wholesale channels for your startup can be a critical decision. To make an informed choice that aligns with your target audience, consider the following factors:

1. Retail:
   Retail involves selling products directly to consumers through physical stores, e-commerce platforms, or other direct channels. Here's why retail might be a suitable option for your startup:

- Engaging with customers: Retail allows you to directly interact with customers, understand their needs, and build strong relationships. This can be particularly valuable if your target audience values personalized experiences and seeks a connection with the brand.
- Showcasing your brand: Through retail, you can create a physical presence for your brand, allowing customers to see, touch, and experience your products firsthand. This can help build trust, create brand awareness, and foster customer loyalty.
- Flexibility in pricing and promotions: Retail empowers you to set your own prices and run promotional campaigns, giving you the flexibility to attract and retain customers.

However, keep in mind the potential challenges of the retail channel:

- Higher operational costs: Establishing and maintaining retail stores can involve significant expenses, including rent, utilities, and staffing. Ensure that your business model and financial projections can support these costs.
- Inventory management complexities: Retail requires effective inventory management to balance stock levels and meet customer demands without overstocking or stockouts. Implement systems or technologies to streamline this process.
- Intense competition: Retail is a highly competitive space, with many businesses vying for customers' attention. Conduct thorough market research

to identify your unique selling points and develop strategies to differentiate yourself from competitors.

2. Wholesale: Wholesale involves selling products in larger quantities to other businesses or retailers who then sell them to end consumers. Consider the following aspects when contemplating the wholesale channel:

- Scaling sales volume: Wholesale allows you to reach a broader customer base by selling larger quantities to retailers or businesses. This can lead to higher sales volumes and potential revenue growth.
- Streamlined distribution: Working with wholesalers can simplify your distribution process, as they can help you reach a wider network of retailers. This can save you time and effort in managing individual sales relationships.
- Cost savings: Wholesalers often offer discounted prices for bulk purchases, allowing businesses to save on per-unit costs. This can be advantageous if your target audience values affordability and cost-effectiveness.

However, bear in mind the potential downsides of wholesale:

- Lower profit margins: Wholesale prices are typically lower than retail prices, which can impact your profit margins. Ensure you have a clear understanding of your cost structure and calculate the profitability of wholesale transactions.
- Limited control over branding and customer experience: As your products are sold to other businesses, you may have less control over how your brand is presented and the overall customer experience. Maintain open communication with your wholesale partners to align on brand guidelines and expectations.
- Building strong partnerships: Success in wholesale relies on establishing and maintaining strong relationships with wholesalers. Invest time and effort in finding reliable partners who align with your values and business goals.

Remember, your decision should align with your target audience's preferences and behaviors. Conduct market research, analyze customer demographics, and consider factors such as price sensitivity, brand perception, and demand patterns. Additionally, you may explore a hybrid approach, combining both retail and wholesale strategies, to leverage the benefits of each channel and cater to different customer segments.

✓ **Chapter 9: Understanding the Importance of SWOT Analysis**

SWOT analysis is a powerful tool that helps entrepreneurs gain valuable insights into their business and make informed decisions. It involves evaluating the strengths, weaknesses, opportunities, and threats that impact the company's performance. By conducting a SWOT analysis, entrepreneurs can uncover internal and external factors that affect their business and develop strategies to capitalize on strengths, overcome weaknesses, seize opportunities, and mitigate threats.

Evaluating *Strengths, Weaknesses, Opportunities, and Threats*

When evaluating strengths, entrepreneurs identify the internal factors that give their business a competitive advantage. This could include unique skills, expertise, valuable assets, or a strong brand reputation. Weaknesses, on the other hand, are internal factors that hinder business growth, such as lack of resources, limited market presence, or outdated technology.

Opportunities refer to external factors that can be leveraged to the business's advantage. These could be emerging market trends, untapped customer segments, or technological advancements. Threats are external factors that pose challenges or risks to the business, such as intense competition, changing consumer preferences, or economic uncertainties.

Developing a Business Plan Based on SWOT Analysis

A business plan is a comprehensive document that outlines the goals, strategies, and operational details of a business. It provides a roadmap for success and helps entrepreneurs communicate their vision to stakeholders. By incorporating the insights gained from a SWOT analysis into the business plan, entrepreneurs can develop a robust strategy that aligns with their strengths, addresses weaknesses, capitalizes on opportunities, and mitigates threats.

A business plan based on SWOT analysis ensures that entrepreneurs have a clear understanding of their competitive position in the market, the target market they want to serve, and the strategies needed to achieve their business objectives. It helps them make informed decisions, allocate resources effectively, and adapt to changing market conditions.

In conclusion, understanding the importance of SWOT analysis empowers entrepreneurs to evaluate their business objectively and develop a business plan that maximizes their strengths, minimizes weaknesses, seizes opportunities, and mitigates threats. It serves as a foundation for strategic decision-making and positions the business for long-term success.

Case study Maria's Knitwear

Maria is a young mother of two who has a passion for knitting. She wants to turn her hobby into a business and sell her knitting products. Let's analyze each word of the SWOT framework and how Maria can utilize it:
1. Strengths: Strengths are internal factors that give a business an advantage over others. For Maria, some potential strengths could be:
- Knitting expertise: Maria's skill and experience in knitting can set her apart from competitors.
- Unique designs: If Maria creates unique and innovative knitting patterns or products, it can attract customers who are looking for something distinct.

- Personal touch: As a young mother, Maria can incorporate her personal story and values into her knitting brand, connecting with customers who appreciate handmade and heartfelt products.

To make the most of her strengths, Maria should emphasize them in her marketing materials, communicate the value they bring to customers, and leverage them to differentiate her business from competitors.

2. Weaknesses: Weaknesses are internal factors that place a business at a disadvantage. Some potential weaknesses for Maria's knitting business could be:
- Limited production capacity: If Maria can only produce a limited number of knitting products due to time constraints, it could be a challenge to meet high customer demand.
- Limited marketing experience: If Maria lacks knowledge or experience in marketing and promoting her products, it may hinder her ability to reach a wider audience.

To address weaknesses, Maria can consider strategies like improving her time management skills, seeking support or outsourcing certain tasks, and investing time in learning about effective marketing techniques.

3. Opportunities: Opportunities are external factors that can benefit a business. For Maria, there may be several opportunities:
- Growing demand for handmade products: In recent years, there has been a resurgence of interest in handmade and artisanal products, which presents an opportunity for Maria to tap into a growing market.
- Online selling platforms: Utilizing e-commerce platforms and social media can help Maria reach a broader audience and expand her customer base beyond her local area.

To seize opportunities, Maria can focus on building a strong online presence, participating in craft fairs or local events, and leveraging social media to showcase her knitting products.

4. Threats: Threats are external factors that can potentially harm a business. Some threats that Maria may face include:
- Intense competition: The market for knitting products can be competitive, with many other sellers offering similar products.
- Fluctuating market trends: Customer preferences and trends in the knitting industry may change, impacting demand for specific types of products.

To address threats, Maria can conduct regular market research to stay informed about trends, explore niche markets or unique product offerings, and strive for continuous improvement and innovation in her designs.

By conducting a thorough SWOT analysis, Maria can gain insights into her knitting business, identify areas to capitalize on, and develop strategies to mitigate weaknesses and threats. This analysis will help her make informed decisions and position her business for success.

Now it's time to write your SWOT:

SWOT

Strengths
Internal factor

Weaknesses
Internal factor

Opportunities
external factor

Threats
External factor

✓ **Chapter 10: Building a Strong Brand**

The Power of Branding in Small Business

Branding plays a vital role in the success of small businesses. It goes beyond just a logo and encompasses the overall perception, values, and identity of a company. Effective branding helps businesses stand out in a crowded market, establish credibility, and build strong relationships with customers. It's a powerful tool that enables entrepreneurs to create a unique and memorable impression in the minds of their target audience.

Creating a Memorable Logo and Strapline

A logo serves as the visual representation of a brand and should be carefully designed to reflect the essence of the business. It should be simple, distinctive, and memorable. Alongside the logo, a strapline or tagline can communicate the brand's unique value proposition and leave a lasting impact on customers. Together, they form a powerful combination that helps differentiate the business from competitors and create brand recognition.

Selecting Colors and Design Elements

Colors and design elements are crucial in creating a cohesive and visually appealing brand identity. The choice of colors can evoke specific emotions and resonate with the target audience. Design elements, such as typography, shapes, and graphics, should align with the brand's personality and values. Consistency in the use of colors and design elements across all brand materials helps reinforce brand recognition and establish a strong visual identity.

Communicating Ethical Values

In today's business landscape, consumers increasingly seek brands that align with their ethical values. Communicating ethical values in branding helps build trust and loyalty among customers. It involves transparently conveying the brand's commitment to social responsibility, sustainability, fair practices, and community involvement. By doing so, small businesses can attract like-minded customers who resonate with their values and beliefs.

Establishing Consistency Across All Brand Touchpoints

Consistency is key when it comes to branding. Every interaction or touchpoint a customer has with the brand should reflect a consistent and unified message. This includes everything from the website and social media profiles to packaging, customer service, and marketing materials. Consistency fosters brand recognition, builds trust, and ensures a seamless and cohesive brand experience for customers.

In conclusion, harnessing the power of branding is essential for small businesses. It involves creating a memorable logo and strapline, selecting appropriate colors and design elements, communicating ethical values, and establishing consistency across all brand touchpoints. By investing in strong branding, entrepreneurs can differentiate their business, connect with their target audience, and build a brand that leaves a lasting impression.

1. **Define your brand identity:**

   Brand identity is the combination of visual and verbal elements that represent your business. It includes your brand name, logo, color palette, typography, imagery, and tone of voice.

   It's essential to define your brand's personality, values, and positioning. Consider how you want your brand to be perceived by your target audience.

   Your brand identity should align with your business's core values, products, and overall mission. It should differentiate you from competitors and create a lasting impression on your audience.

   - Analyze your target audience, including their preferences, values, and needs. This will help you shape your brand's personality and positioning.
   - Create a mission statement that clearly communicates your brand's purpose and values.
   - Develop a unique selling proposition (USP) that sets your brand apart from competitors.
   - Design a brand logo, color palette, and visual elements that align with your brand identity.

   Pros of doing it on your own: You have full creative control and can customize your brand identity according to your vision. Cons of doing it on your own: It may be challenging to create a professional and cohesive brand identity without expertise in design and branding principles.

2. **Craft your brand message:**

   Your brand message is the core essence of what your business offers and the value it provides to customers. It goes beyond just product features and focuses on the emotional and functional benefits.

   Develop a unique selling proposition (USP) that sets your brand apart from competitors. This is a clear statement that highlights what makes your business unique and why customers should choose you.

   Your brand message should resonate with your target audience and evoke the desired emotions, whether it's trust, excitement, or reliability.

   - Clearly articulate what your brand offers and the benefits it provides to customers.
   - Develop a compelling and consistent brand voice that resonates with your target audience.
   - Craft a tagline or slogan that encapsulates your brand's essence.

   Pros of doing it on your own: You intimately understand your business and can create a genuine brand message. Cons of doing it on your own: It can be difficult to effectively communicate your brand message without professional copywriting skills.

3. **Build brand awareness:**

    Brand awareness is the level of recognition and familiarity that your target audience has with your brand. It involves creating visibility and exposure for your business.

    Establish an online presence through a well-designed website and active social media profiles. Consistently share valuable content that aligns with your brand and engages your audience.

    Utilize content marketing strategies such as blogging, videos, and social media posts to educate, inspire, and entertain your audience.

    Implement search engine optimization (SEO) techniques to improve your brand's visibility in search engine results.

    - Establish an online presence through a website and social media profiles.
    - Use content marketing strategies, such as blogging and social media posting, to share valuable and relevant information with your audience.
    - Leverage search engine optimization (SEO) techniques to improve your brand's visibility in search engine results.

    Pros of doing it on your own: You have direct control over your online presence and can engage with your audience directly. Cons of doing it on your own: Building brand awareness requires expertise in digital marketing, and it can be time-consuming to implement and optimize strategies.

4. **Consistency across touchpoints:**

    Brand consistency is crucial for building trust and recognition. Ensure that your brand identity, messaging, and visuals are consistent across all platforms and marketing materials.

    Use your brand's visual elements consistently, including the logo, colors, typography, and imagery, in your website, social media profiles, packaging, and advertisements.

    Deliver a consistent brand experience through excellent customer service, product quality, and brand interactions at every touchpoint.

    - Ensure your brand identity and messaging are consistent across all platforms and marketing materials.
    - Use consistent visual elements, such as logos, colors, and typography, in your website, social media profiles, packaging, and advertisements.
    - Deliver a consistent brand experience through excellent customer service and product quality.

    Pros of doing it on your own: You can maintain complete control over the brand consistency and ensure it aligns with your vision. Cons of doing it on your own: Consistently applying branding across various touchpoints can be challenging without a deep understanding of brand management principles.

5. **Monitor and adapt:**

    Regularly monitor the performance of your branding efforts using various metrics, such as website traffic, social media engagement, and customer feedback.

Gather insights from your target audience and adapt your branding strategy based on their preferences, market trends, and feedback. Continuously refine and improve your brand to stay relevant and meet the evolving needs of your audience.

- Regularly assess the effectiveness of your branding efforts using metrics like website traffic, social media engagement, and customer feedback.
- Adapt your branding strategy based on market trends, customer preferences, and feedback to stay relevant and competitive.

Pros of doing it on your own: You have direct insights into your brand's performance and can quickly make adjustments. Cons of doing it on your own: Without expertise in data analysis and market research, it may be challenging to accurately interpret and act upon the data.

*What no one will tell you about Marketing:

Marketing is more than just promoting your product or service. It's about telling a compelling story that resonates with your audience. Share the story behind your brand, the passion, the purpose, and the values that drive you. Let your customers connect with the authentic narrative, forming a bond that goes beyond a transaction. Remember, it's not just your story, but the story behind your product/service that truly captivates hearts and minds.

Case Study Maria's Knitwear

Maria is a young mother of three who creates handmade knitting products. She wants to establish her brand and reach a wider audience. Here's how she can apply the above instructions:

1. Define her brand identity by selecting appropriate visual elements that represent her business, such as a unique brand name, a visually appealing logo, a harmonious color palette, and suitable typography. Maria used pastel pink and handwritten typography, as her target audience is mostly mums and women.
2. Craft a compelling brand message that highlights the emotional and functional benefits of her handmade knitting products, emphasizing aspects like quality, craftsmanship, and the personal touch. On her labels is emphasized that all products are handknitted by her in her small house workshop.
3. Build brand awareness by creating a professional website that showcases her products and their unique features. Utilize social media platforms, such as Instagram or Pinterest, to share captivating visuals of her knitting creations and engage with her target audience. Maria knows that her real customers are not family and friends. She is reaching our a wider audience by using a professional website with high-quality photos, that showcase her products.
4. Maintain consistency across all touchpoints by ensuring her brand identity, messaging, and visuals remain consistent on her website, social media

profiles, packaging, and customer interactions. Packaging is always the same, following the brand's colors and typography. This also creates a sense of trust unlikely with her competitors who use different packaging each time, by buying from different suppliers and seaking out for offers.

5. Monitor the performance of her branding efforts by analyzing website analytics, social media metrics, and customers behavior. Maria is using analytics and adjusts accordingly offers, new products promotions and newsletter content.

✓ **Chapter 11: Designing a Successful Logo**

Let's analyze the role of the logo in more detail and discuss the pros and cons of new entrepreneurs attempting to create it themselves instead of hiring an expert:

***Designing a logo that represents your brand*:**
The logo is a visual representation of your brand and serves as a powerful tool for brand recognition. Creating a logo that accurately represents your brand values, personality, and target audience is crucial.

Pros:
- Cost-saving: Designing the logo yourself can save money, especially for entrepreneurs with limited budgets.
- Creative control: You have complete creative control over the design process, allowing you to align the logo with your vision.

Cons:
- Lack of expertise: Designing a professional and visually appealing logo requires a certain level of design knowledge and skill. Without experience, it can be challenging to create a high-quality logo.
- Time-consuming: Developing a logo from scratch can be time-consuming, particularly if you're not familiar with design software or techniques. This can divert your focus from other important business tasks.

Using online logo makers or templates:
Online logo makers and templates provide pre-designed elements that can be customized to create a logo.

Pros:
- Ease of use: Online logo makers offer user-friendly interfaces and step-by-step guidance, making it easier for non-designers to create a logo.
- Cost-effective: Many online logo makers offer free or affordable options, making it a budget-friendly choice.

Cons:
- Lack of uniqueness: Templates and pre-designed elements can result in generic-looking logos, which may not effectively differentiate your brand.
- Limited customization: While online logo makers provide customization options, they may have limitations in terms of fonts, colors, and overall design flexibility.

Seeking feedback and iterating:
It's important to gather feedback on your logo and iterate based on the input received.

Pros:
- Feedback from target audience: Seeking feedback allows you to understand how your logo is perceived by your target audience and make necessary improvements.
- Cost-saving: Iterating on your logo design based on feedback is a cost-effective approach compared to starting from scratch.

Cons:
- Limited external perspective: As a solo entrepreneur, you may not have access to diverse opinions and design expertise. This can limit the range of feedback and potentially hinder the development of a strong logo.

Considering professional design assistance:
Hiring a professional designer or agency to create your logo can ensure a high-quality and visually appealing result.

Pros:
- Expertise and creativity: Professional designers possess the skills, knowledge, and experience to create visually stunning and effective logos that resonate with your target audience.
- Time-saving: Outsourcing the logo design process frees up your time, allowing you to focus on other aspects of your business.

Cons:
- Cost: Hiring a professional designer or agency can be more expensive compared to creating the logo yourself.
- Communication challenges: Working with a designer requires effective communication to ensure your vision and brand values are accurately translated into the logo design.

In summary, while there are benefits to creating a logo on your own, such as cost savings and creative control, it's important to consider the potential drawbacks, including a lack of expertise and time consumption. Hiring a professional designer can ensure a high-quality and unique logo, but it may come with additional costs and communication challenges. Ultimately, the decision should be based on your budget, design skills, and the importance you place on having a strong and distinctive brand identity.

*What no one will tell you about brand identity:
Branding is more than just a logo. It's about how you consistently present your brand through visuals, messaging, packaging, and customer experience.

✓ **Chapter 12: Understanding Costs and Profit Margin**

Costs involved in producing a knitted pullover:
To ensure a comprehensive understanding of costs, new entrepreneurs like Mary should consider the following:
- Cost of materials (e.g., yarn, knitting needles, buttons): Mary should determine the exact costs for each component used in creating a single knitted pullover.

- Labor costs: Mary needs to estimate the number of hours it takes to knit a pullover and assign a reasonable hourly rate. This ensures that her time and effort are accounted for as a cost.
- Overhead expenses: Mary should identify any additional expenses related to her business, such as packaging materials, shipping costs, and marketing expenses.
- Miscellaneous costs: It's important for Mary to consider any other incidental costs, such as transaction fees for online sales or fees associated with selling at craft fairs.

Calculating profit margin:
Profit margin is a crucial metric for evaluating the profitability of a product. Mary can calculate the profit margin using the following formula:
Profit Margin = ((Selling Price - Total Costs) / Selling Price) * 100
By subtracting the total costs (including materials, labor, overhead, and miscellaneous costs) from the selling price, dividing it by the selling price, and multiplying by 100, Mary can determine the profit margin as a percentage. This helps her assess the profitability of each knitted pullover she sells.

Determining retail and wholesale prices:
_When it comes to setting prices for her knitted pullovers, Mary should consider the following factors:

- Retail price: Mary needs to consider her target market, competitors' pricing, and the perceived value of her products. By adding the total costs per pullover (including materials, labor, overhead, and miscellaneous costs) to the desired profit margin, she can determine the retail price that covers her expenses and ensures profitability.
- Wholesale price: If Mary intends to sell her pullovers to retailers or other resellers, she should establish a wholesale price that allows for a profit margin while offering an attractive price for retailers to earn their interest.

Now let's apply these principles to Mary's case study: Mary purchases her knitting supplies, including yarn and buttons, for £10 per pullover. She estimates that it takes her 5 hours to knit a pullover, and she values her time at £15 per hour. Therefore, the labor cost for one pullover is £75 (5 hours x £15 per hour). Additionally, Mary accounts for £5 in overhead expenses, which include packaging materials and shipping costs. The total cost per pullover is calculated as follows:

Total Costs = Cost of materials + Labor costs + Overhead expenses Total Costs = £10 + £75 + £5 = £90

To ensure a reasonable profit margin, Mary decides to aim for a 40% profit margin on the selling price. Using the profit margin formula, Mary can calculate the selling price that would yield this desired profit margin:

Profit Margin = ((Selling Price - Total Costs) / Selling Price) * 100 40 = ((Selling Price - £90) / Selling Price) * 100

41

Solving the equation, we find: Selling Price - £90 = 0.4 * Selling Price 0.6 * Selling Price = £90 Selling Price = £90 / 0.6 = £150

Therefore, Mary should set her retail price at $150 per knitted pullover.

WHOLESALE PRICING

If Mary wants to sell her knitted pullovers at wholesale prices, she needs to consider a different pricing strategy. Typically, wholesale prices are lower than retail prices to incentivize retailers to purchase in bulk. Here's how Mary can determine her wholesale price:

1. Calculate the desired profit margin: Mary should decide on a reasonable profit margin for her wholesale transactions. This margin will be lower than the retail profit margin since she is offering a discounted price to retailers.
2. Determine the wholesale discount: Mary needs to determine the percentage discount she is willing to offer to wholesale buyers. Common wholesale discounts range from 40% to 60%, depending on the industry and product.
3. Calculate the wholesale price: To calculate the wholesale price, subtract the wholesale discount from the retail price. This discounted price ensures that Mary still earns a profit while offering retailers a competitive price.

For example, if Mary decides to offer a 50% wholesale discount on her knitted pullovers, she can calculate the wholesale price as follows:

Wholesale Price = Retail Price - (Retail Price * Wholesale Discount) Wholesale Price = £150 - (£150 * 0.5) Wholesale Price = £150 - £75 Wholesale Price = £75

Therefore, Mary should set her wholesale price at £75 per knitted pullover. This price accounts for the wholesale discount while still allowing her to make a profit on each wholesale transaction.

✓ **Chapter 13: Product Packaging or Presentation for Services**

Packaging plays a crucial role in the success of a product. It not only protects the item during transportation and storage but also serves as a powerful tool for branding and marketing. As an entrepreneur, choosing the right packaging supplier is a critical decision that can impact various aspects of your business. One important consideration is whether to source packaging from China or opt for local suppliers. Each option comes with its own set of advantages and disadvantages that must be carefully weighed. In this article, we will explore the pros and cons of both approaches to help you make an informed decision that aligns with your business goals and target audience. Let's delve into the world of packaging and discover which sourcing option may be the most suitable for your specific needs.

In service-based businesses, packaging refers to the way services are presented, delivered, and perceived by customers. While physical packaging is more commonly associated with product-based businesses, service packaging focuses on the intangible aspects that shape the overall customer experience. It encompasses various elements that contribute to the delivery and presentation.

Case study George Personal Trainer

For example, let's consider George, a 35-year-old single professional tennis player who also works as a personal trainer. As a personal trainer, George's service packaging goes beyond just providing fitness training. It encompasses several elements that enhance the overall customer experience and differentiate him from his competitors.

Firstly, George focuses on personalization. He tailors his training programs to meet the specific needs, goals, and fitness levels of his clients. By taking the time to understand each client's individual requirements, he can provide customized workouts and coaching that are more effective and engaging.

Secondly, George emphasizes professionalism. He maintains a high level of expertise and stays updated with the latest trends and research in the fitness industry. This ensures that he delivers quality training sessions and accurate information to his clients. Additionally, he maintains a professional demeanour, punctuality, and clear communication, which builds trust and reliability.

Furthermore, George leverages his professional tennis background to add value to his service packaging. He incorporates tennis-specific techniques, agility drills, and mental conditioning exercises into his training programs. This unique offering sets him apart from other personal trainers and attracts tennis enthusiasts who are seeking specialized training.

Additionally, George pays attention to the overall presentation of his services. He maintains a professional website and social media presence that showcases his credentials, client testimonials, and success stories. This online presence serves as virtual packaging, allowing potential clients to get a glimpse of his expertise and the results he has achieved for his clients.

By focusing on these aspects of service packaging, George creates a compelling and differentiated offering. His personalized approach, professionalism, and tennis expertise appeal to his target audience and position him as a trusted and sought-after personal trainer in his area.

Overall, service packaging in the context of personal training and service-based businesses involves customizing services to meet individual needs, maintaining professionalism and expertise, leveraging unique skills or backgrounds, and presenting services in a way that builds trust and attracts the target audience.

Here's an analysis of the pros and cons of sourcing packaging from big wholesalers like Alibaba, and DHgate versus local suppliers:

Sourcing packaging from China:

Pros:

1. Cost-effectiveness: Chinese manufacturers often offer competitive pricing due to lower labour and production costs.
2. Wide variety and customization options: China has a vast range of packaging options, allowing customization and flexibility to meet specific product needs.
3. Scale and capacity: Chinese suppliers can handle large volume orders, making them suitable for businesses with high-demand products.
4. International shipping expertise: Chinese manufacturers are experienced in exporting goods globally, ensuring smooth shipping processes and compliance with import/export regulations.

Cons:

1. Longer lead times: Shipping products from China generally takes longer than sourcing locally, which can impact delivery schedules and inventory management.
2. Communication and language barriers: Working with Chinese suppliers may involve language challenges and potential miscommunication, requiring extra effort in clarifying requirements.
3. Quality control risks: Distance and limited oversight may make it more challenging to ensure product quality and address issues promptly.
4. Intellectual property concerns: There can be risks associated with protecting intellectual property rights when working with overseas suppliers.

Sourcing packaging from local suppliers:

Pros:

1. Faster turnaround times: Working with local suppliers can significantly reduce lead times, enabling quicker product launches and order fulfilment.
2. Easier communication and coordination: Being in the same geographical area allows for easier communication, faster response times, and the ability to visit suppliers in person if necessary.
3. Quality control and oversight: Local suppliers can be easily monitored, allowing for greater control over product quality and the ability to address any issues promptly.

4. Supporting local businesses: Sourcing locally contributes to the local economy and may resonate with customers who prioritize supporting local businesses.

Cons:

1. Higher costs: Local suppliers may have higher manufacturing and labor costs, resulting in potentially higher packaging prices.
2. Limited customization options: Local suppliers may offer fewer options for customizing packaging compared to manufacturers in China.
3. Capacity constraints: Local suppliers may have limited production capacity, making it challenging to meet large volume orders.
4. Reduced global reach: If your business has international customers, sourcing locally may limit your ability to expand into global markets efficiently.

When deciding between sourcing packaging from China or local suppliers, consider factors such as budget, product requirements, delivery timelines, and the potential impact on your brand image. It's essential to assess the pros and cons in relation to your specific business needs and objectives before deciding.

✓ **Chapter 14: Financing Your Business**

When starting a new business, one of the crucial aspects to consider is sourcing the necessary funds to turn your ideas into reality. As a new entrepreneur targeting the small-micro business segment, there are several potential sources of financing that you can explore. Let's delve into some of these options:

- **Personal Savings:** This is often the first and most accessible source of funds for many new entrepreneurs. Utilizing your own savings demonstrates your commitment and belief in your business idea. Consider evaluating your personal finances and determine how much you can invest in your venture.
  Pros:
  Accessible and convenient, demonstrates commitment, and retains control over the business.
  Cons:
  Limited funds available, personal financial risk, the potential strain on personal finances.

- **Friends and Family:** Another common option is to seek financial support from friends and family members who believe in your business vision. This can be in the form of a loan or an investment. Be sure to establish clear terms and expectations to maintain healthy relationships.
  Pros:
  Easier to secure funds, potential for more flexible terms, and supportive network.
  Cons:
  Strained relationships if the business faces challenges, potential conflicts over money, and limited funds available.

- **Bootstrapping:** Bootstrapping involves starting and growing your business with minimal external funding. This approach requires careful financial management, cutting unnecessary costs, and fully utilizing existing resources. While it may require more time and effort, bootstrapping allows you to maintain control over your business and avoid debt.

Pros:
Retains complete control, no debt or interest payments, resourceful and efficient use of existing assets.

Cons:
Slow growth, limited initial investment, reliance on personal resources.

- **Crowdfunding:** Crowdfunding platforms provide an opportunity to raise funds from a large number of people who believe in your business idea. Create a compelling campaign, showcase your products or services, and offer attractive rewards or incentives to backers. Platforms like Kickstarter and Indiegogo are popular for crowdfunding campaigns.

Pros:
Access to a large pool of potential backers, validation of the business idea, marketing and exposure.

Cons:
Time-consuming to create and manage a campaign, competitive environment, rewards or equity obligations.

- **Small Business Loans:** Explore options for small business loans from banks, credit unions, or online lenders. These loans typically require a solid business plan, financial projections, and collateral or a personal guarantee. Research the available loan programs and compare terms, interest rates, and repayment schedules to find the most suitable option.

Pros:
Access to larger amounts of capital, flexible repayment terms, and potential for building business credit.

Cons:
Stringent eligibility criteria, collateral or personal guarantee required, interest payments and debt.

- **Grants and Competitions:** Look for grants, business competitions, and incubator programs that provide funding and support for new businesses. These opportunities often require a well-crafted business plan and a compelling pitch to secure financial backing. Research local and national programs that are specific to your industry or target audience.

Pros:
Non-repayable funds, validation of the business concept, access to mentorship and resources.

Cons:
Highly competitive, time-consuming application process, limited availability and specific eligibility criteria.

- **Microfinance Institutions:** Microfinance institutions specialize in providing small loans to entrepreneurs, especially those in underserved communities. They focus on supporting businesses that may not qualify for traditional bank loans. Research microfinance institutions in your area and determine their eligibility criteria and loan terms.

Pros:
Designed for underserved entrepreneurs, with smaller loan amounts available, and flexible repayment terms.
Cons:
Higher interest rates, smaller loan sizes, and limited availability in certain regions.

- **Supplier Financing:** Some suppliers offer financing options to their customers, allowing you to purchase inventory or equipment with flexible payment terms. This can help manage cash flow during the initial stages of your business.

Pros:
Flexible payment terms help manage cash flow, and builds relationships with suppliers.
Cons:
Limited to purchasing from specific suppliers, potential impact on profit margins, dependency on supplier relationships.

- **Angel Investors:** Angel investors are individuals or groups who provide capital and mentorship to early-stage businesses in exchange for equity or a return on investment. Seek out angel investor networks or attend startup events to network and pitch your business idea.

Pros:
Access to capital and expertise, potential network and industry connections, and shared business risk.
Cons:
Dilution of ownership, loss of some control, and finding the right investor fit can be challenging.

- **Government Programs and Support:** Investigate government programs, grants, and initiatives aimed at supporting small businesses and startups. These can include tax incentives, subsidies, or low-interest loans designed to encourage entrepreneurship and economic growth.

Pros:
Financial incentives, grants or loans with favourable terms, and business development resources.
Cons:
Strict eligibility criteria, bureaucratic processes, limited availability for specific industries or regions.

- **Pre-order finance:** A pre-order finance option is a method of funding a business where customers place orders and make payments for products or services before they are officially released or produced. This allows the business to generate revenue upfront, which can be used to cover production

47

costs and other expenses associated with bringing the product or service to market.

Pros:

1. Cash flow: Pre-orders provide an immediate influx of cash to the business, helping to cover upfront expenses and reduce reliance on external funding sources.
2. Market validation: Pre-orders serve as a strong indicator of market demand and customer interest. If there is a high volume of pre-orders, it demonstrates that there is a market for the product or service.
3. Customer engagement: Pre-orders create anticipation and excitement among customers, fostering a sense of involvement and loyalty to the brand or product.
4. Reward opportunities: Pre-orders can be incentivized with rewards or benefits, such as discounted prices, exclusive access, or special privileges for early supporters.

Cons:

1. Production challenges: Meeting customer expectations and delivering on pre-orders can be challenging, especially if there are delays or unforeseen issues in the production process.
2. Refund obligations: If the business fails to deliver the promised product or service, it may result in customer dissatisfaction and refund requests, which can impact the business's reputation and finances.
3. Uncertain demand: While pre-orders can indicate market interest, they are not always a guarantee of sustained demand once the product or service is released. There is still a risk that customer interest may wane after the initial pre-order phase.
4. Cash flow timing: Since pre-orders are collected upfront, the business may need to manage its cash flow carefully to ensure it has the necessary funds to fulfill customer orders while covering ongoing operational expenses.

When considering a pre-order finance option, it's important for entrepreneurs to carefully evaluate their business model, production capabilities, and customer demand. They should also communicate transparently with customers about the pre-order process, including potential risks and timelines. By offering rewards or incentives for pre-orders, such as discounts or exclusive membership benefits, entrepreneurs can further enhance customer engagement and encourage early support for their business.

It's important to carefully evaluate each financing option based on your specific business needs and goals. Consider factors such as the amount of funds required, repayment terms, impact on ownership and control, and the potential risks involved. Additionally, consider seeking professional advice from a business advisor or financial expert to help you make informed decisions.

Remember, the financing option you choose should align with your long-term business objectives and support sustainable growth.

<u>*Can you guess which financial method I used?</u>

<u>*Hint: I started my business having only £500, and with no help from friends or family as I had just moved to a new country. (This business four years later was rocking six figures, eight awards and a retail store).</u>

What no one will tell you about financing options: Don't limit yourself to traditional bank loans. No bank will give a loan to a startup unless there is a strong business plan. Look for alternatives, like pre-orders and crowdfunding.

CHAPTER 15: BUSINESS PLAN

A business plan is a comprehensive document that outlines the goals, strategies, and financial projections for a new or existing business. It serves as a roadmap for entrepreneurs, guiding them in making informed decisions, securing funding, and achieving their business objectives. A well-crafted business plan is crucial for both startups and established businesses, as it provides a clear direction and increases the likelihood of success.

Importance of a Business Plan:

1. Clarity of Vision: A business plan helps you define and articulate your business idea, mission, and vision, providing a clear understanding of what you want to achieve.
2. Goal Setting: It enables you to set specific, measurable, achievable, relevant, and time-bound (SMART) goals for your business, allowing you to track progress and make necessary adjustments.
3. Strategic Planning: A business plan helps you develop strategies and action plans to achieve your goals, including marketing, operations, financial, and growth strategies.
4. Financial Planning: It allows you to forecast revenue, expenses, and cash flow, helping you determine the financial viability of your business and attract investors or secure loans.
5. Risk Assessment: By conducting a thorough analysis of market trends, competition, and potential challenges, a business plan helps identify and mitigate risks.
6. Funding and Investor Pitching: A well-written business plan increases your chances of obtaining financing from banks, investors, or venture capitalists, as it demonstrates a solid understanding of your business and its potential for success.
7. Communication and Team Alignment: A business plan serves as a communication tool, ensuring that all stakeholders, including employees,

partners, and advisors, are aligned with your business objectives and strategies.

How to Write a Business Plan on Your Own:

1. Executive Summary: Provide a concise overview of your business, highlighting its unique value proposition, target market, and financial projections.
2. Company Description: Describe your business, its legal structure, mission, vision, and core values.
3. Market Analysis: Conduct market research to identify your target market, analyze industry trends, competition, and customer needs.
4. Product or Service Offering: Clearly define your products or services, including their features, benefits, and unique selling points.
5. Marketing and Sales Strategies: Outline your marketing and sales strategies to reach and attract your target audience, including pricing, distribution, and promotional tactics.
6. Organizational Structure: Define the organizational structure of your business, including key personnel, their roles and responsibilities, and their qualifications.
7. Financial Projections: Prepare financial forecasts, including income statements, balance sheets, and cash flow statements, for at least three years. Include assumptions and break-even analysis.
8. Funding Request: If seeking funding, clearly state the amount of funding required, how it will be used, and potential sources of funding.
9. Implementation Plan: Detail the steps and timeline for executing your business strategies, including milestones and key performance indicators (KPIs).
10. Risk Assessment: Identify potential risks and challenges that may affect your business and develop strategies to mitigate them.

Pros of Writing a Business Plan on Your Own:

1. Cost Savings: Creating a business plan on your own eliminates the need to hire a professional writer or consultant, saving money.
2. In-Depth Understanding: Writing your own business plan allows you to gain a comprehensive understanding of your business and its various aspects.
3. Customization: You have the flexibility to tailor the business plan to suit your specific business model and goals.

Cons of Writing a Business Plan on Your Own:

1. Time-Consuming: Writing a thorough business plan requires significant time and effort, especially if you're new to the process.
2. Limited Expertise: Without professional guidance, you may overlook important components or fail to present the information effectively.
3. Lack of Objectivity: Writing your own business plan may

BUSINESS PLAN TEMPLATE

Here's a basic business plan template for small businesses:

1. Executive Summary
   - Briefly summarize your business idea, mission, target market, and financial projections. Add your logo and business details.
2. Company Description
   - Provide an overview of your company, including its legal structure, location, and history.
   - Explain your business model, products or services, and unique value proposition.
   - Share your mission statement and core values.
3. Market Analysis
   - Describe your target market, including its size, demographics, and purchasing behavior.
   - Analyze the competition and identify your competitive advantages.
   - Research industry trends, market growth potential, and any regulatory or economic factors that may impact your business.
4. Product or Service Offering
   - Describe your products or services in detail, including their features, benefits, and pricing.
   - Explain how your offerings fulfil customer needs and solve their problems.
   - Highlight any unique selling points or competitive advantages.
5. Marketing and Sales Strategy
   - Outline your marketing and sales approach to reach and engage your target audience.
   - Identify your marketing channels, such as social media, website, advertising, or partnerships.
   - Define your pricing strategy and sales tactics, including distribution channels and customer acquisition methods.
6. Organizational Structure and Management
   - Describe the legal structure of your business (e.g., sole proprietorship, partnership, LLC).
   - Outline the roles and responsibilities of key team members and their qualifications.
   - Discuss your hiring plan, including future staffing needs and any strategic partnerships or outsourcing plans.
7. Financial Projections
   - Create a detailed financial forecast, including income statements, balance sheets, and cash flow projections for at least three years.
   - Estimate your startup costs, ongoing expenses, and revenue projections.
   - Include a break-even analysis and key financial ratios to demonstrate the financial viability of your business.
8. Funding Request (if applicable)
   - If seeking funding, clearly state the amount of funding required and how it will be used.

- Explain your repayment plan and potential sources of funding, such as loans, grants, or investor contributions.
9. Implementation Plan
   - Detail your action plan for executing your business strategies and achieving your goals.
   - Set milestones and timelines to track progress and measure success.
   - Identify any risks or challenges and outline contingency plans.
10. Appendix
   - Include any supporting documents, such as resumes, licenses, permits, market research data, or legal agreements.

Remember, this template is just a starting point, and you can customize it to fit your specific business needs.

What no one will tell you about writing a business plan: Don't get caught up in overly complex jargon. Keep your plan concise, easy to understand, and focused on the key aspects of your business. Use colors and typography to match your branding.

Chapter 16: Building and Engaging Through Social Media

Social media has become an indispensable tool for businesses in today's digital age. It offers a powerful platform to connect with customers, build brand awareness, and drive engagement. In this chapter, we will explore the key strategies for harnessing the power of social media and effectively engaging your audience.

Harnessing the Power of Social Media for Business

Social media platforms provide an immense opportunity for businesses to reach a wide audience and promote their products or services. By creating a strong presence on platforms such as Facebook, Instagram, Twitter, and LinkedIn, you can establish your brand's voice and connect with potential customers. It's important to understand the demographics and preferences of your target audience to determine which platforms will yield the best results for your business.

Creating Engaging Content

One of the most effective ways to captivate your audience on social media is by creating engaging content. This involves crafting posts that are not only informative but also entertaining, interesting, and shareable. Consider diversifying your content by including a mix of posts showcasing your products, giving a glimpse into your brand story, sharing funny or relatable content, hosting interactive games or quizzes, and offering exciting giveaways. Experiment with different formats such as images, videos, and live streams to keep your audience engaged.

Utilizing Keywords and Hashtags

To maximize the reach and visibility of your social media posts, it's crucial to utilize keywords and hashtags effectively. Research and identify the keywords and hashtags that resonate with your target audience and align with your products or services. Incorporate them strategically into your posts to increase discoverability and join relevant conversations. This will help your content appear in search results and reach a wider audience interested in your industry or niche.

Consistency in Branding

Maintaining consistency in your branding across social media platforms is essential for building a strong and recognizable brand identity. Ensure that your profile pictures, cover photos, color schemes, typography, and tone of voice align with your overall brand image. Consistency helps create brand recognition and fosters trust among your audience. Craft a cohesive brand story and narrative that reflects your values and resonates with your target customers.

The Importance of Daily Presence and Engagement

Consistency and active engagement are key to building a thriving social media presence. Dedicate time each day to post relevant content, respond to comments and messages, and engage with your audience. Encourage conversations, ask questions, and listen to your customers' feedback. Engaging with your audience not only strengthens relationships but also helps gather insights and valuable feedback to improve your products or services.

Algorithms: What They Are and How to Train Them

Social media platforms use algorithms to determine which content appears on users' feeds. Understanding how algorithms work can significantly impact your social media strategy. While the exact workings of algorithms may be complex and constantly evolving, you can optimize your content by focusing on engagement metrics such as likes, comments, and shares. Encourage your audience to interact with your posts, and create content that sparks meaningful conversations and generates genuine interest.

In conclusion, social media is a powerful tool for businesses to connect with their audience, build brand awareness, and drive engagement. By creating engaging content, utilizing keywords and hashtags, maintaining consistency in branding, and being present and engaged daily, you can effectively leverage social media to grow your business. Additionally, understanding algorithms and adapting your content strategy accordingly can help maximize your reach and visibility on social media platforms. Embrace the opportunities social media offers and watch your business thrive in the digital landscape.

*What no one will tell you about social media:
Consistency is key. Regularly post engaging content, interact with your audience,
and stay up to date with the latest social media trends and features. This is also

crucial when you are working with a social media manager, to make sure they have consistent posting and engagement.

As you approach the launch of your business, it's crucial to have the following essential elements in place:

1. **Trademark Availability and Registration:**
   - Conduct thorough research to check the availability of your desired business name as a trademark.
   - Consult with a legal professional specializing in intellectual property to secure the trademark if it's available.
   - Protecting your business name through trademark registration helps establish brand recognition and prevents others from using a similar name.
2. **Financial Management and Accounting:**
   - Consult with an experienced accountant or financial advisor to set up a robust financial tracking system for your business.
   - Implement accounting software or tools to effectively manage income, expenses, and cash flow.
   - Regularly track and review financial statements to monitor the health of your business and make informed decisions.
3. **Marketing Strategy and Launch Plan:**
   - Develop a comprehensive marketing strategy that outlines your target audience, key messaging, and promotional activities.
   - Conduct market research to identify the most effective channels and tactics to reach your target audience.
   - Create a launch plan that includes specific goals, timelines, and action steps to generate buzz and attract customers during the launch phase.
4. **Business Operations Setup:**
   - Determine the appropriate setup for your business operations based on your industry and target market.
   - If it's a physical store, secure a location, and set up the necessary infrastructure and equipment.
   - For an online shop, establish a user-friendly website, implement secure payment gateways, and ensure smooth order fulfilment and shipping processes.
   - In the case of a service-based setup, define your service offerings, and pricing structure, and establish efficient scheduling and client management systems.
5. **Legal Compliance and Licensing:**
   - Register your business entity with the appropriate government authorities based on your location and business structure (e.g., sole proprietorship, Ltd etc).
   - Research and obtain any necessary licenses or permits required for your industry and geographical location.
   - Ensure compliance with local, state, and federal regulations related to taxes, employment, and operations.

54

By having these essential elements in place, you can set a strong foundation for your business and increase your chances of success. It is recommended to consult with professionals, such as trademark attorneys, accountants, and business advisors, to ensure that you navigate these aspects effectively.

Here is a general list of the steps you need to do to start:

1. Define your business idea: Identify your unique product or service and determine how it solves a problem or fulfils a need in the market.

2. Conduct market research: Understand your target audience, competitors, and industry trends. Gather insights to shape your business strategy.

3. Develop a business plan: Outline your goals, objectives, and strategies. Include financial projections, marketing plans, and operational details.

4. Build your brand: Create a compelling brand identity, including a logo, website, and marketing materials that reflect your unique value proposition.

5. Set up your infrastructure: Establish necessary systems, such as accounting, inventory management, and customer relationship management, suppliers sourcing.

6. Register your business: Choose a legal structure and complete the necessary paperwork to establish your business entity.

7. Secure funding: Determine your financial needs and explore funding options such as self-funding, loans, grants, or investors.

8. Launch your marketing efforts: Develop a marketing plan to reach your target audience through various channels, both online and offline.

9. Establish sales channels: Determine the best ways to sell your products or services, whether through e-commerce, local markets, physical stores, or wholesale partnerships.

10. Provide exceptional customer service: Prioritize customer satisfaction and build strong relationships to encourage repeat business and positive word-of-mouth.

Conclusion:

Congratulations on taking the first steps toward becoming a successful entrepreneur. "Start and Succeed" provides you with the knowledge and guidance you need to navigate the complexities of starting a small business. Remember, the road to success may be challenging, but with dedication, strategic planning, and a strong brand, you can build a thriving business that stands the test of time. Dream big and act small, and may your entrepreneurial journey be filled with fulfillment and prosperity.

If I made it, anyone could make it!

Manifest and believe !

Want to get in touch and discuss your business idea? I am more than excited to hear about it. Click here: https://smallbusinessadvisor.uk/